the dog intelligence test

CARTOONS
Mike Scovel, *Houston Chronicle*

ILLUSTRATIONS AND CARTOONS
Ted Ohtani, Studio O
Box 77, Oliver Springs, Tennessee

DESIGN
Based on the original design by
Dwight Agner, Baton Rouge, Louisiana

PHOTOGRAPHS
Bill Feig, Jr., Baton Rouge *Morning Advocate*

KATHY COON

the dog intelligence test

 AVON
PUBLISHERS OF BARD, CAMELOT AND DISCUS BOOKS

AVON BOOKS
A division of
The Hearst Corporation
959 Eighth Avenue
New York, New York 10019

First Avon Printing, March, 1978

CONTENTS

Kathy Coon tests Daiquiri

DOG INTELLIGENCE TEST

INTRODUCTION

Daiquiri, a potential obedience school dropout, was always belittled by family and friends as the "world's dumbest dog." "I really didn't think Daiquiri could be all *that* dumb," said Kathy Coon, who developed the Dog Intelligence Test to find out her canine's capabilities.

Daiquiri's performance was compared with over one hundred dogs who had taken the test, and guess what! Daiquiri wasn't so dumb after all—in fact Daiquiri was of average intelligence! These results caused significant changes in Daiquiri's behavior: Now Daiquiri not only chases her tail, she catches it!

Kathy Coon holds a master's degree in psychology and has been a dog owner for twenty-five years. With this pedigree behind her, she developed the test with Tender Loving Care and designed it to be enjoyable for you and your dog.

PURPOSE

The Dog Intelligence Test will give you and your dog a chance to have fun and will allow you to compare your dog with over one hundred dogs who have taken the test. This test is not designed to predict how well your dog will do in specific skills or in obedience school. Instead, it is designed to give an overall picture of how much your dog understands in comparison with other dogs who have been tested.

FREQUENTLY ASKED QUESTIONS
ABOUT THE TEST

Q. What does the test consist of?

A. The test is made up of ten separate tests which are given in order in one test session. Total time is between fifteen and twenty minutes.

Q. What do the tests show?

A. Tests 1 through 5 show your dog's ability to remember where objects are placed. These tests also show how quick your dog is in shifting attention. Tests 6 and 7 show agility and ability to adapt. Tests 8 and 9 show your dog's ability to solve normal and unique detour problems. Test 10 shows how quickly your dog reacts to conditions which he or she finds unacceptable.

2

Q. How hard is each test?

A. The best way to answer this question is to show the percentage of dogs passing each test.

Percentage of Dogs
Passing Tests

Test 1=51%   Test 6=44%
Test 2=69%   Test 7=61%
Test 3=65%   Test 8=73%
Test 4=50%   Test 9=66%
Test 5=53%   Test 10=46%

Q. How old does your dog have to be?

A. If your dog is to do well, he or she must be at least twelve weeks old. (Younger dogs are not mature enough for testing.)

3

Q. When should the tests be given?

A. Test at a time convenient to you and your dog. Dogs who have just been fed do not generally do their best, so test your dog at some other time.

Q. Where should the tests be given?

A. Test your dog in a comfortable and familiar place.

Q. Who should give the test?

A. Two people are needed for testing. One person, the **Caller,** will call and actually test the dog. The second person, the **Holder,** will hold the dog on some tests, return the dog to position between tests, and record how the dog does using the Score Sheet provided. Some dogs will do better with the owner as **Caller;** others, with the owner as **Holder.** Since you want your dog to do his or her best, you must decide which arrangement is best for your dog.

Q. Is there any way to tell how well your dog will do on the test?

A. Yes. There is a significant relationship between the number of tricks your dog can do (for example, "can come when ordered"; "can sneeze or bark when ordered," etc.) and how smart your dog is measured to be on the Dog Intelligence Test. This suggests that the more tricks your dog knows the more likely the dog is to do well on this test.

Q. Does early toilet training predict how well your dog will do?

A. No. As with people on intelligence tests, early toilet training does not suggest that your dog will do well.

Q. Does your estimate of your dog's intelligence predict how well your dog will do?

A. No. Actually, results strongly suggest that if you think your dog is smart the dog is likely to do less well than you expect, and if you think your dog is dumb the dog is likely to do better.

WHAT YOU WILL NEED
TO TEST YOUR DOG

To properly test your dog you will need a watch with a second hand, this book, the Score Sheet, and a pencil. These materials will be used for each of the ten tests.

In addition you will need:
> Three identical plastic cups or bowls (margarine tubs would do fine) for Tests 1–5.
> A box of dog treats for Tests 1–7.
> A standard-size shoebox for Tests 6 and 7.
> A rubber ball for Test 8.
> A chair with a crossbar low enough so that your dog cannot go under it for Test 8.
> A beach towel for Tests 9 and 10. If you have a medium or large dog, substitute a twin-size bed-sheet for Test 10.

Before testing your dog, the following preparations should be made using the above materials:

For Test 6, you should cut a 2×2 inch square hole in *one* of the long sides of the shoebox, as shown in Figure 1.

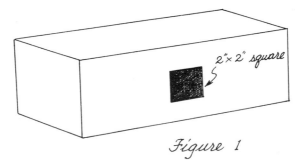

2″×2″ square

Figure 1

For Test 7, you should make a ⅛ inch cut in one of the bottom corners of the shoebox lid, as shown in Figure 2.

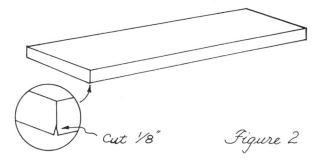

Cut ⅛"   *Figure 2*

For Test 9, The beach towel should be attached securely at the top between a door frame, across a hallway or between two doors, as shown in Figure 3.

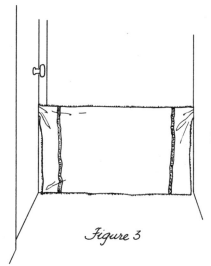

Figure 3

1. For small dogs the top of the towel should be one foot off the ground.
2. For medium-size and large dogs the top of the towel should be two feet off the ground.

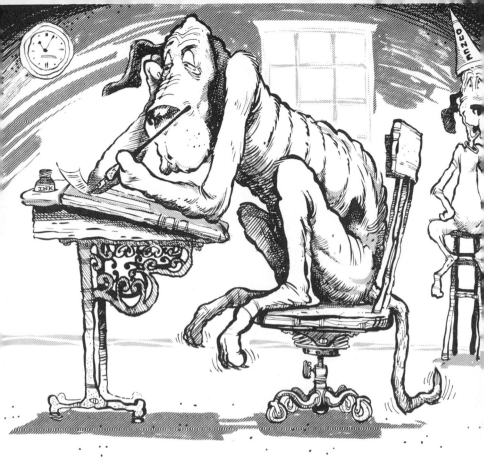

GIVING THE TEST

Once you have the above equipment prepared as outlined, you will be ready to test. It is advisable to practice all ten tests once without your dog to become familiar with them. You should read the entire procedure and study the Score Sheet thoroughly before testing your dog. If you feel that it would be better to substitute a toy for a dog treat or vice versa for any of the tests, feel free to do so. The **Holder** should copy or remove the Score Sheet from the book and record how the dog does after each test.

Tests 1–5

Materials needed:

> Test book
> Three plastic cups
> Dog treats
> Score Sheet
> Watch
> Pencil

Tests 1–5 are similar. For each test the cups should be arranged as indicated in Figure 4. The cups should be placed upside down about six inches apart. The **Holder** should hold the dog by the collar about four feet back from the middle cup. The **Caller** should sit, facing the dog, on the other side of the middle cup.

The **Caller** should put a treat under the cup on his left (cup 1 in Figure 4). This treat is not to be removed until Test 5 is completed.

 Holder's position

Dog

○   ○   ○

Cup 1   *Cup 2*   *Cup 3*

⊕ *Caller's position*

Figure 4

Test 1

The **Caller** should have another treat in his hand. He should hold the treat two inches above cup 3, calling the dog's attention to the treat and then swiftly placing it under cup 3. He then calls the dog.

After a wait of 30 seconds, the **Holder** should release the dog. To pass the test, the dog must go directly to cup 3 (not to another cup or to owner first) in 15 seconds or less. The test is completed the moment the dog goes to any cup or directly to the **Caller.** The **Caller** removes the treat, and the **Holder** records how the dog does on the Score Sheet.

Do not let the dog turn over the cups. However, if the dog goes directly to cup 3, you may feed your dog a treat. Return the dog to the holder position after the test is completed.

Tests 2 and 3

Tests 2 and 3 are similar to Test 1. Test 1 directions should be followed *exactly* except the treat is placed under cup 2 instead of under cup 3 for both Tests 2 and 3. If your dog did not pass Test 1, the dog may be fed a treat on the next test passed.

Test 4

Test 1 directions should be followed *exactly* for Test 4, except the treat is placed under cup 3, and you should not feed the dog.

Test 5

Test 1 directions should be followed *exactly* for Test 5, except the **Caller** places the treat under cup 1. There should now be two treats under cup 1 because one treat should have been there since the first test. If the dog passes, give the dog a treat.

Test 6

Materials needed:
> Test book
> Shoebox (without the lid)
> Treat
> Score Sheet
> Watch
> Pencil

For this test the dog does not need to be held. Place the shoebox (without the lid) upside down on the floor as seen in the photograph.

The **Caller** holds a treat in his hand. He then calls the dog and lets the dog sniff the treat. He immediately places the treat under the box. The **Holder** starts timing. Encourage the dog in every possible way to retrieve the treat. To pass, your dog must retrieve the treat from the shoebox in 15 seconds or less. To get the treat the dog does not need to turn the box over, but it is okay if he does so. Stop the test if the dog goes beyond 15 seconds and let him or her have the treat.

World's Greatest Dog

This certifies that _____
Dog's Name

was administered the Dog Intelligence

Test on _____ by _____ .
Date _Examiner_

Performance on this test suggests

that not only is this dog very much

loved but is also _____ .
Level of Intelligence

I hereby state that the test was

given according to instructions, and the results

were in keeping with the aforementioned performance.

_____   _____
Signed   Date

Test 7

Materials needed:

> Test book
> Shoebox with lid
> Treat
> Score Sheet
> Watch
> Pencil

For this test the dog does not need to be held. Place the treat in the shoebox with your dog watching. Put the lid on the shoebox immediately by placing the slit lid ½ inch from the edge of the box so that the box side fits into the ⅛ inch slit. (This will secure the box lid to the shoebox.) See Figure 5.

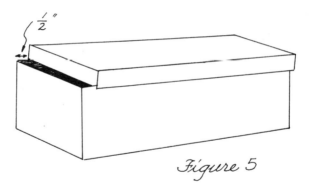

Figure 5

The **Holder** starts timing immediately. Encourage the dog to do his or her best to obtain the treat. If the dog loses interest, tap the box (side only) and call the dog to the shoebox. To pass, your dog must retrieve the treat from the shoebox in 15 seconds or less. The lid need not be off completely. Stop the test if your dog goes beyond 15 seconds. Give the treat to your dog.

Test 8

Materials needed:

> Test book
> Chair with low cross bars
> Ball
> Score Sheet
> Watch
> Pencil

Play ball with the dog. At some point in the play, roll the ball under the chair with low cross bars. Figure 6 shows some of the acceptable ways to roll the ball.

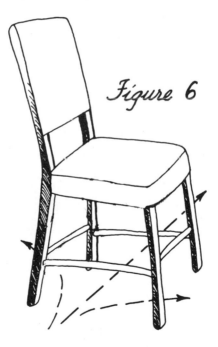

Figure 6

To pass, your dog must go *directly* to the ball in 15 seconds or less. If your dog goes to the chair first, the dog fails. Stop the test if your dog goes beyond 15 seconds.

Note: If you don't roll the ball properly on your first try, play more ball with your dog and try until you do.

Test 9

Materials needed:
> Test book
> Beach towel
> Ball
> Score Sheet
> Watch
> Pencil

The **Caller** takes the ball and goes to the other side of the beach towel which has been attached between a door frame or two doorways (see photograph). The **Caller** stands back from the towel about two feet. The dog is held about four feet from the towel, facing the **Caller,** who is on the other side of the towel. The **Caller** then bounces the ball twice behind the beach towel. The ball should be bounced high enough to be seen by your dog. The dog is called and then encouraged to reach the **Caller.** The **Holder** immediately releases the dog and starts timing.

To pass, your dog must reach the **Caller** in 15 seconds or less. Your dog may go either under or over the towel. Stop the test if your dog goes beyond 15 seconds.

Test 10

Note: If this test will upset or excite your dog, do not give it.
Instead score as directed.

Materials needed:
>Test book
>Beach towel (a twin bedsheet is substituted for the beach towel for medium-size and large dogs)
>Score Sheet
>Watch
>Pencil

Put the towel over the dog and wrap it around your dog clockwise. (Do not tuck the towel under your dog.) The **Holder** starts timing immediately after the dog is wrapped and stops when the dog is completely out of the towel. Encourage the dog to come out as quickly as possible. To pass, your dog must be completely freed from the towel in 15 seconds or less. Stop the test and unwrap your dog if your dog goes beyond 15 seconds.

Scoring

Do you recall that you should have copied or removed the Score Sheet from pages 27–28 before testing your dog? For each test you should indicate the time in seconds in the space provided on the Score Sheet and indicate *pass* or *fail*. To pass any test your dog must do what is required within 15 seconds.

After completing the Score Sheet for Tests 1–10, count the total number of passes earned by your dog for all ten tests. This number is your dog's **Total Score.**

Note: If you did not give Test 10 add one point to your dog's total only if your dog obtained a Total Score of 5 or more. Otherwise, the score is the same.

If your dog earned
a **Total Score** *of* 0–2   Your dog is **Very Dumb**
                    3–4   Your dog is **Dumb**
                    5–7   Your dog is **Average**
                    8   Your dog is **Smart**
                    9   Your dog is **Very Smart**
                    10   Your dog is **Brilliant**

These scores are based on over 100 dogs that have taken this test (Average score=5.75; standard deviation=1.1).

If you wish to fill out the certificate in the book, the **bold-faced words** in the right-hand column of this table indicate your dog's level of intelligence.

The following information may be of help in interpreting your dog's score.

Male dogs are slightly smarter than female dogs (Male average=6.10; female=5.55).

Mixed breeds are about as smart as pure breeds (mixed breed=5.80; Pure breed average=5.98).

Some groups of purebred dogs do slightly better than others. For example, Hounds, Non-sporting, and Sporting dogs (Hound average=7.63; Non-sporting=6.33; Sporting=6.17) tend to do better than Working, Terrier, and Toy dogs (Working average=5.67; Terrier average=5.25; Toy average=4.78).

FOR YOUR INFORMATION

In the original sample population there were an equal number of male and female dogs, purebred and mixed breed dogs, registered and non-registered purebred dogs, breed dogs of the six groups recognized by the American Kennel Club (Sporting Dogs, Hounds, Working Dogs, Terriers, Toys, Non-sporting Dogs), and small, medium-sized and large dogs. Obedience-trained and non-trained dogs and dogs of various ages were also tested. Although no statistically significant differences in performance on the Dog Intelligence Test were obtained among any of the above groups, the following information may be of help in interpreting your dog's score.

Male dogs are slightly smarter than female dogs (Male average=6.10; Female=5.55).

Mixed breeds are about as smart as pure breeds (Mixed breed average=5.80; Pure breed average=5.98).

Among the six groups of dogs recognized by the American Kennel Club, some groups of purebred dogs do slightly better than others. For example, Hounds, Non-sporting, and Sporting dogs (Hound average=7.63; Non-Sporting=6.33; Sporting=6.17) tend to do better than Working, Terrier, and Toy dogs (Working average=5.67; Terrier average=5.25; Toy average=4.78).

Regarding the validity of the Dog Intelligence Test, items were developed to measure the constructs researchers in the psychological literature established as characteristic of intelligence in dogs. With respect to test reliability, a limited sample of dogs were administered the test on several occasions with generally similar results.

Congratulations!

Your dog is *very* fortunate to have an owner who realizes that dogs are the world's greatest pets. Although some dogs may not have done well on the Dog Intelligence Test, the most intelligent owners will realize the special qualities of their own dogs.

SCORE SHEET

(Copy or remove from Book)

General Scoring Rules

1. On Tests 1–5 **Holder** must hold dog for *exactly* 30 seconds after the dog is called before releasing dog.
2. The dog has only 15 seconds to complete each of the ten tests. If the dog takes 16 or more seconds, the test is failed.
3. Rewards can be treats or play activities. Rewards should be given as follows:
   For Tests 1–3 reward the dog on the first pass. For Test 4 there is no reward. If the dog passes Test 5, give the dog a treat. For Tests 6 and 7 the dog gets the treat used in the tests.

Summary of Instructions for Each Test

Record the Following

	Time	Pass	Fail
Test 1 — Caller calls dog. Holder holds dog 30 seconds, then releases dog and starts timing.	____	____	____
Test 2 — Caller calls dog. Holder holds dog 30 seconds, then releases dog and starts timing.	____	____	____
Test 3 — Caller calls dog. Holder holds dog 30 seconds, then releases dog and starts timing.	____	____	____
Test 4 — Caller calls dog. Holder holds dog 30 seconds, then releases dog and starts timing.	____	____	____
Test 5 — Caller calls dog. Holder holds dog 30 seconds, then releases dog and starts timing.	____	____	____

To pass Tests 1–5, the dog must go to the correct cup first (not to another cup or to owner) in 15 seconds or less.

Test 6   Treat is put in shoebox.
Immediately start timing.   _____   _____   _____

*To pass Test 6, the dog must retrieve the treat from the shoebox
in 15 seconds or less. The shoebox need not be turned over.*

Test 7   Lid is put on the
shoebox. Immediately
start timing.   _____   _____   _____

*To pass Test 7, the dog must retrieve the treat from the shoebox
in 15 seconds or less. The lid need not be off.*

Test 8   Ball is rolled under
chair. Immediately start
timing.   _____   _____   _____

*To pass Test 8, the dog must go directly to the ball in 15 sec-
onds or less. If the dog goes to the chair first, the dog fails.*

Test 9   Caller calls dog. Holder
releases dog im-
mediately and starts tim-
ing.   _____   _____   _____

To pass Test 9, the dog must reach the **CALLER** *in 15 seconds or
less. The dog may go either under or over the towel.*

Test 10   Dog is wrapped. Im-
mediately start timing.   _____   _____   _____

*To pass Test 10, the dog must be completely freed from the
towel in 15 seconds or less.*

Count the total number of passes earned by the dog for all ten
tests. This number is the dog's **Total Score,** referred to on page
42 of the manual.

PEOPLE PERSONALITY PROFILE DEVELOPED BY YOUR FAVORITE DOG

Note: Dogs have not had the benefit of formal psychometric training. As such the test is somewhat subjective. Nevertheless it represents a first in recognition of canine capabilities.

PEOPLE PERSONALITY PROFILE
SCORE SHEET

(Copy or remove from Book)

Please remember that your dog is giving you the test. Therefore, "you" refers to you, the owner, and "me," "my," etc., refer to the dog.

Check the response that applies most to you.

Yes   **No**

<u>Yes</u>   <u>No</u>   **1.**   You anticipate my needs.

<u>Yes</u>   <u>No</u>   **2.**   You walk well on a leash.

<u>Yes</u>   <u>No</u>   **3.**   You are a good sport.

<u>**Yes**</u>   <u>**No**</u>   **4.**   You are gentle with children.

<u>Yes</u>   <u>No</u>   **5.**   You are well trained.

<u>Yes</u> <u>No</u> **6.** You protect our happy home.

<u>Yes</u> <u>No</u> **7.** You look better every day.

<u>Yes</u>   <u>No</u>   **8.**   You only choose the best.

<u>Yes</u>   <u>No</u>   **9.**   You are obedient.

<u>**Yes**</u>   <u>**No**</u>   **10.**   You are entertaining.

<u>**Yes**</u>   <u>**No**</u>   **11.**   You are lovable.

<u>**Yes**</u> <u>**No**</u> **12.** You understand my every desire.

<u>**Yes**</u> <u>**No**</u> **13.** You allow me to make my own friends.

36

__Yes__ __No__ **14.** You scare away strangers.

__Yes__ __No__ **15.** You are a good traveling companion.

__Yes__ __No__ **16.** You are well bred.

__Yes__ __No__ **17.** You heel well.

38

<u>Yes</u> <u>No</u> **18.** You have an extensive dog vocabulary.

<u>Yes</u> <u>No</u> **19.** You come when called.

__Yes__ __No__ **20.** You express yourself well.

__Yes__ __No__ **21.** You know it's never too late.

Count the number of yes responses checked. This number is your **Total Score,** referred to on page 41.

PEOPLE PERSONALITY PROFILE

LEVEL OF PERSONALITY

If you obtained a
Total Score of

0–10 Your level of personality is **Sad**

11–15 Your level of personality is **Satisfactory**

16–21 Your level of personality is **Superb**

If you wish to fill out the certificate in the book, the **bold-faced words** in the right hand column of this table indicate your level of personality.

People always want to know how compatible they and their dog are.

Now you can find out from the

PEOPLE PERSONALITY PROFILE

A Compatibility Chart Prepared by
Your Favorite Dog

Directions:
Obtain your and your dog's **Total Score.** Find where they merge in the following table. You will then know how compatible you are.

COMPATIBILITY CHART

	Your Total Score		
	0–10	11–15	16–21
Your Dog's Total Score			
0	Compatible	Compatible	Most Compatible
1	Compatible	Compatible	Most Compatible
2	Compatible	Compatible	Most Compatible
3	Compatible	Compatible	Most Compatible
4	Compatible	Compatible	Most Compatible
5	Incompatible	Compatible	Most Compatible
6	Incompatible	Compatible	Most Compatible
7	Incompatible	Compatible	Most Compatible
8	Incompatible	Compatible	Most Compatible
9	Incompatible	Compatible	Most Compatible
10	Incompatible	Compatible	Most Compatible

Dog's Best Friend

This certifies that _____
                        Owner's Name
was administered the People-Personality
Profile on _____ by _____.
              Date   Dog's Name
Performance on this test suggests that not
only is this owner very much loved but is also

_____.
Level of Personality

I hereby state that the test was given
according to instructions, and the results
were in keeping with the aforementioned
performance.

_____   _____
Paw Print   Date

TABLE OF BREEDS

Group	Breed
Sporting Dogs	
	Pointer
	Retriever, Golden
	Retriever, Labrador
	Setter, Irish
	Spaniel, Cocker
	Spaniel, English Springer
Hounds	
	Afghan Hound
	Basset Hound
	Beagle
	Dachshund (smooth-coated)
	Whippet
Working Dogs	
	Belgian Tervuren
	Boxer
	Collie
	Doberman Pinscher
	German Shepherd Dog
	Great Dane
	St. Bernard
	Shetland Sheepdog
	Siberian Husky
Terriers	
	Airedale Terrier
	Schnauzer, Miniature
	West Highland White Terrier
Toys	
	Chihuahua (smooth-coated)
	Pekingese
	Pomeranian
	Toy Poodle
	Pug
	Silky Terrier

Non-sporting Dogs
　　　　　Bulldog
　　　　　Lhasa Apso
　　　　　Miniature Poodle
　　　　　Standard Poodle
　　　　　Schipperke

Miscellaneous
　　　　　Australian Shepherd

BREED NORMS

Breed norms were developed after the original standardization using additional dogs. These norms will not give you a definitive answer regarding how smart a given breed is since small numbers of dogs were used for the comparison samples. The norms are not intended to replace the overall rating of your dog's intelligence but rather to provide a context for it.

Now that you have found out how much your dog understands in comparison with other dogs who have been tested, you may want to know how well your dog stacks up to dogs of the same breed used in the subsequent breed sample. The breed index will serve as your guide for comparison.

Available representative and popular breeds were selected for developing these norms. While not all breeds are listed, the data will provide a comparison for your dog. For example, Chihuahuas (long-coated) could feel fairly comfortable in using Chihuahua (smooth-coated) norms. Different questions were asked regarding different breeds due to the limitations of formal statistics.

SPORTING DOGS

POINTER

Q. How hard is each test for Pointers?

A. The best way to answer this is to show the percentage of Pointers passing each test.

Percentage of Tests Passed

Test 1=50%	**Test 6**=80%
Test 2=35%	**Test 7**=85%
Test 3=20%	**Test 8**=90%
Test 4=55%	**Test 9**=80%
Test 5=45%	**Test 10**=50%

Q. How well do Pointers do?

A. The average score is 5.9 with a standard deviation of 1.4.

Q. How smart is your dog in comparison to other Pointers?

A. If your dog obtained a total score of

0–3	Your dog is a very dumb Pointer
4	Your dog is a dumb Pointer
5–7	Your dog is an average Pointer
8–9	Your dog is a smart Pointer
10	Your dog is a brilliant Pointer

Q. How do the sexes stack up?

A. There are no differences between Pointer males and females.

RETRIEVER, GOLDEN

Q. How hard is each test for Golden Retrievers?

A. The best way to answer this is to show the percentage of Golden Retrievers passing each test.

Percentage of Tests Passed

Test 1=80%	**Test 6**=85%
Test 2=70%	**Test 7**=90%
Test 3=75%	**Test 8**=95%
Test 4=60%	**Test 9**=75%
Test 5=75%	**Test 10**=70%

Q. How well do Golden Retrievers do?

A. The average score is 7.9 with a standard deviation of 1.8.

Q. How smart is your dog in comparison to other Golden Retrievers?

A. If your dog obtained a total score of

0–4   Your dog is a very dumb Golden Retriever
5–6   Your dog is a dumb Golden Retriever
7–9   Your dog is an average Golden Retriever
10   Your dog is a brilliant Golden Retriever

Q. How do the sexes stack up?

A. There are no differences between Golden Retriever males and females.

RETRIEVER, LABRADOR

Q. How hard is each test for Labrador Retrievers?

A. The best way to answer this is to show the percentage of Labrador Retrievers passing each test.

Percentage of Tests Passed

Test 1=38%	**Test 6**= 88%
Test 2=63%	**Test 7**= 88%
Test 3=38%	**Test 8**= 88%
Test 4=63%	**Test 9**=100%
Test 5=50%	**Test 10**= 88%

Q. How well do Labrador Retrievers do?

A. The average score is 5.6 with a standard deviation of 2.9.

Q. How smart is your dog in comparison to other Labrador Retrievers?

A. If your dog obtained a total score of

0–2	Your dog is a dumb Labrador Retriever
3–9	Your dog is an average Labrador Retriever
10	Your dog is a brilliant Labrador Retriever

Q. How do the sexes stack up?

A. Labrador Retriever males are significantly smarter than Labrador Retriever females.

Q. Are city Labs smarter than rural Labs?

A. Yes. City Labs are significantly smarter than rural Labs on the Dog Intelligence Test.

Q. Are registered Labrador Retrievers smarter than non-registered purebred Labs?

A. Results of the Dog Intelligence Test suggest that those registered dogs tested performed significantly better than non-registered purebred Labrador Retrievers. There was greater variation in performance for the non-registered Labs than those registered.

Q. Do the number of dogs in the dwelling relate to how well Labrador Retrievers do on the Dog Intelligence Test?

A. No. There is no relationship between the number of dogs in the dwelling and how well Labrador Retrievers do on the test.

SETTER, IRISH

Q. How hard is each test for Irish Setters?

A. The best way to answer this is to show the percentage of Irish Setters passing each test.

Percentage of Tests Passed

Test 1=30%	**Test 6**=50%
Test 2=35%	**Test 7**=45%
Test 3=40%	**Test 8**=65%
Test 4=25%	**Test 9**=55%
Test 5=40%	**Test 10**=50%

Q. How well do Irish Setters do?

A. The average score is 4.4 with a standard deviation of 2.3.

Q. How smart is your dog in comparison to other Irish Setters?

A. If your dog obtained a total score of

0–2	Your dog is a dumb Irish Setter
3–7	Your dog is an average Irish Setter
8–9	Your dog is a smart Irish Setter
10	Your dog is a brilliant Irish Setter

Q. How do the sexes stack up?

A. There are no differences between Irish Setter males and females.

SPANIEL, COCKER

Q. How hard is each test for Cocker Spaniels?

A. The best way to answer this is to show the percentage of Cocker Spaniels passing each test.

Percentage of Tests Passed

Test 1=50%	**Test 6**=80%
Test 2=30%	**Test 7**=80%
Test 3=20%	**Test 8**=90%
Test 4=50%	**Test 9**=90%
Test 5=40%	**Test 10**=40%

Q. How well do Cocker Spaniels do?

A. The average score is 5.7 with a standard deviation of 1.5.

Q. How smart is your dog in comparison to other Cocker Spaniels?
A. If your dog obtained a total score of

0–2   Your dog is a very dumb Cocker Spaniel
3–4   Your dog is a dumb Cocker Spaniel
5–7   Your dog is an average Cocker Spaniel
8–9   Your dog is a smart Cocker Spaniel
10   Your dog is a brilliant Cocker Spaniel

Q. How do the sexes stack up?

A. There are no differences between Cocker Spaniel males and females.

Q. Are city Cockers smarter than rural Cockers?

A. No. There are no differences between city Cockers and rural Cockers.

Q. Do the number of dogs in the dwelling relate to how well Cocker Spaniels do on the Dog Intelligence Test?

A. No. There is no relationship between the number of dogs in the dwelling and how well Cocker Spaniels do on the test.

Q. Do Cockers who live in the house do better than those who live outside?

A. No. There are no differences in performance.

Q. Do show Cocker Spaniels do better than others?

A. No. There are no differences in performance.

Q. Do housebroken Cocker Spaniels do better than others?

A. No. There are no differences in performance.

SPANIEL, ENGLISH SPRINGER

Q. How hard is each test for English Springer Spaniels?

A. The best way to answer this is to show the percentage of English Springer Spaniels passing each test.

Percentage of Tests Passed

Test 1=70%	**Test 6**=85%
Test 2=80%	**Test 7**=80%
Test 3=75%	**Test 8**=95%
Test 4=65%	**Test 9**=95%
Test 5=80%	**Test 10**=85%

Q. How well do English Springer Spaniels do?

A. The average score is 8.0 with a standard deviation of 1.3.

Q. How smart is your dog in comparison to other English Springer Spaniels?

A. If your dog obtained a total score of

0–5	Your dog is a very dumb English Springer Spaniel
6	Your dog is a dumb English Springer Spaniel
7–9	Your dog is an average English Springer Spaniel
10	Your dog is a brilliant English Springer Spaniel

Q. How do the sexes stack up?

A. There are no differences between English Springer Spaniel males and females.

HOUNDS

AFGHAN HOUND

Q. How hard is each test for Afghan Hounds?

A. The best way to answer this is to show the percentage of Afghan Hounds passing each test.

Percentage of Tests Passed

Test 1=25%	**Test 6**=55%
Test 2=15%	**Test 7**=30%
Test 3=15%	**Test 8**=60%
Test 4=15%	**Test 9**=50%
Test 5=40%	**Test 10**=50%

Q. How well do Afghans do?

A. The average score is 3.5 with a standard deviation of 2.3.

Q. How smart is your dog in comparison to other Afghan Hounds?

A. If your dog obtained a total score of

0–1	Your dog is a dumb Afghan Hound
2–6	Your dog is an average Afghan Hound
7–8	Your dog is a smart Afghan Hound
9–10	Your dog is a brilliant Afghan Hound

Q. How do the sexes stack up?

A. There are no differences between Afghan Hound males and females.

BASSET HOUND

Q. How hard is each test for Basset Hounds?

A. The best way to answer this is to show the percentage of Basset Hounds passing each test.

Percentage of Tests Passed

Test 1=72%	**Test 6**=84%
Test 2=72%	**Test 7**=92%
Test 3=76%	**Test 8**=96%
Test 4=60%	**Test 9**=68%
Test 5=80%	**Test 10**=48%

Q. How well do Basset Hounds do?

A. The average score is 7.5 with a standard deviation of 1.0.

Q. How smart is your dog in comparison to other Basset Hounds?

A. If your dog obtained a total score of

0–5	Your dog is a very dumb Basset Hound
6	Your dog is a dumb Basset Hound
7–9	Your dog is an average Basset Hound
10	Your dog is a brilliant Basset Hound

Q. How do the sexes stack up?

A. There are no differences between Basset Hound males and females.

BEAGLE

Q. How hard is each test for Beagles?

A. The best way to answer this is to show the percentage of Beagles passing each test.

Percentage of Tests Passed

Test 1=88%	**Test 6**=96%
Test 2=92%	**Test 7**=88%
Test 3=84%	**Test 8**=92%
Test 4=76%	**Test 9**=96%
Test 5=60%	**Test 10**=68%

Q. How well do Beagles do?

A. The average score for Beagles is 8.3 with a standard deviation of .9.

Q. How smart is your dog in comparison to other Beagles?

A. If your dog obtained a total score of

0–6	Your dog is a very dumb Beagle
7	Your dog is a dumb Beagle
8–9	Your dog is an average Beagle
10	Your dog is a brilliant Beagle

Q. How do the sexes stack up?

A. There are no differences between Beagle males and females.

DACHSHUND (SMOOTH-COATED)

Q. How hard is each test for Dachshunds?

A. The best way to answer this is to show the percentage of Dachshunds passing each test.

Percentage of Tests Passed

Test 1 = 67%	**Test 6** = 83%
Test 2 = 50%	**Test 7** = 100%
Test 3 = 100%	**Test 8** = 100%
Test 4 = 67%	**Test 9** = 83%
Test 5 = 33%	**Test 10** = 67%

Q. How well do Dachshunds do?

A. The average score is 7.3 with a standard deviation of 1.4.

Q. How smart is your dog in comparison to other Dachshunds?

A. If your dog obtained a total score of

0–4	Your dog is a very dumb Dachshund
5	Your dog is a dumb Dachshund
6–9	Your dog is an average Dachshund
10	Your dog is a brilliant Dachshund

Q. How do the sexes stack up?

A. There are no differences between Dachshund males and females.

Q. Are city Dachshunds smarter than rural Dachshunds?

A. No. There are no differences between city Dachshunds and rural Dachshunds.

Q. Do the number of dogs in the dwelling relate to how well Dachshunds do on the Dog Intelligence Test?

A. No. There is no relationship between the number of dogs in the dwelling and how well Dachshunds do on the test.

WHIPPET

Q. How hard is each test for Whippets?

A. The best way to answer this is to show the percentage of Whippets passing each test.

Percentage of Tests Passed

Test 1=20%	**Test 6**= 20%
Test 2= 0%	**Test 7**=100%
Test 3=60%	**Test 8**=100%
Test 4= 0%	**Test 9**=100%
Test 5= 0%	**Test 10**=100%

Q. How well do Whippets do?

A. The average score is 5.2 with a standard deviation of 1.2.

Q. How smart is your dog in comparison to other Whippets?

A. If your dog obtained a total score of

0–2	Your dog is a very dumb Whippet
3	Your dog is a dumb Whippet
4–6	Your dog is an average Whippet
7–8	Your dog is a smart Whippet
9	Your dog is a very smart Whippet
10	Your dog is a brilliant Whippet

Q. How do the sexes stack up?

A. There are no differences between Whippet males and females.

Q. Do the number of dogs in the dwelling relate to how well Whippets do on the Dog Intelligence Test?

A. No. There is no relationship between the number of dogs in the dwelling and how well Whippets do on the test.

Q. Do related dogs (i.e., dogs of the same bloodline) do better or worse than non-related dogs?

A. No. There is no difference in the performance of related and non-related dogs.

WORKING DOGS

BELGIAN TERVUREN

Q. How hard is each test for Belgian Tervurens?

A. The best way to answer this is to show the percentage of Belgian Tervurens passing each test.

Percentage of Tests Passed

Test 1=80%	**Test 6**= 80%
Test 2=40%	**Test 7**=100%
Test 3=60%	**Test 8**=100%
Test 4=40%	**Test 9**=100%
Test 5=20%	**Test 10**=100%

Q. How well do Belgian Tervurens do?

A. The average score is 6.8 with a standard deviation of .75.

Q. How smart is your dog in comparison to other Belgian Tervurens?

A. If your dog obtained a total score of

0–5	Your dog is a very dumb Belgian Tervuren
6	Your dog is a dumb Belgian Tervuren
7–8	Your dog is an average Belgian Tervuren
9	Your dog is a very smart Belgian Tervuren
10	Your dog is a brilliant Belgian Tervuren

Q. How do the sexes stack up?

A. There are no differences between Belgian Tervuren males and females.

Q. Do related dogs (i.e., dogs of the same bloodline) do better or worse than non-related dogs?

A. No. There is no difference in the performance of related and non-related dogs.

BOXER

Q. How hard is each test for Boxers?

A. The best way to answer this is to show the percentage of Boxers passing each test.

Percentage of Tests Passed

Test 1=50%	**Test 6**=50%
Test 2=55%	**Test 7**=60%
Test 3=65%	**Test 8**=80%
Test 4=40%	**Test 9**=65%
Test 5=50%	**Test 10**=50%

Q. How well do Boxers do?

A. The average score is 5.5 with a standard deviation of 1.0.

Q. How smart is your dog in comparison to other Boxers?

A. If your dog obtained a total score of

0–3	Your dog is a very dumb Boxer
4	Your dog is a dumb Boxer
5–7	Your dog is an average Boxer
8	Your dog is a smart Boxer
9	Your dog is a very smart Boxer
10	Your dog is a brilliant Boxer

Q. How do the sexes stack up?

A. There are no differences between Boxer males and females.

COLLIE

Q. How hard is each test for Collies?

A. The best way to answer this is to show the percentage of Collies passing each test.

Percentage of Tests Passed

Test 1=80%	**Test 6**=85%
Test 2=75%	**Test 7**=80%
Test 3=70%	**Test 8**=90%
Test 4=65%	**Test 9**=70%
Test 5=75%	**Test 10**=65%

Q. How well do Collies do?

A. The average score is 7.0 with a standard deviation of 1.6.

Q. How smart is your dog in comparison to other Collies?

A. If your dog obtained a total score of

0–3	Your dog is a very dumb Collie
4–5	Your dog is a dumb Collie
6–9	Your dog is an average Collie
10	Your dog is a brilliant Collie

Q. How do the sexes stack up?

A. There are no differences between Collie males and females.

DOBERMAN PINSCHER

Q. How hard is each test for Doberman Pinschers?

A. The best way to answer this is to show the percentage of Doberman Pinschers passing each test.

Percentage of Tests Passed

Test 1=36%	**Test 6**=36%
Test 2=27%	**Test 7**=68%
Test 3=36%	**Test 8**=86%
Test 4=14%	**Test 9**=82%
Test 5=14%	**Test 10**=77%

Q. How well do Doberman Pinschers do?

A. The average score is 4.7 with a standard deviation of 2.2.

Q. How smart is your dog in comparison to other Doberman Pinschers?

A. If your dog obtained a total score of

0	Your dog is a very dumb Doberman Pinscher
1–2	Your dog is a dumb Doberman Pinscher
3–7	Your dog is an average Doberman Pinscher
8–9	Your dog is a smart Doberman Pinscher
10	Your dog is a brilliant Doberman Pinscher

Q. How do the sexes stack up?

A. There are no differences between Doberman Pinscher males and females.

Q. Are city Dobs smarter than rural Dobs?

A. No. There are no differences between city Dobs and rural Dobs.

Q. Do the number of dogs in the dwelling relate to how well Doberman Pinschers do on the Dog Intelligence Test?

A. No. There is no relationship between the number of dogs in the dwelling and how well Doberman Pinschers do on the test.

Q. Do Dobs who live in the house do better than those who live outside?

A. No. There are no differences in performance.

Q. Do show Dobs do better than others?

A. No. There are no differences in performance.

Q. Do housebroken Doberman Pinschers do better than others?

A. Yes. Housebroken Dobs do significantly better than non-housebroken Dobs.

Q. Do non-kennel Doberman Pinschers do better than kennel dobs?

A. No. There are no differences in performance.

Q. Do related dogs (i.e., dogs of the same bloodline) do better or worse than non-related dogs?

A. Yes. Related dogs' performances were significantly more consistent than non-related dogs' performances.

Q. Do adult Doberman Pinschers do better than puppies?

A. No. There are no differences in performance.

GERMAN SHEPHERD DOG

Q. How hard is each test for German Shepherds?

A. The best way to answer this is to show the percentage of German Shepherds passing each test.

Percentage of Tests Passed

Test 1=55%	**Test 6**=50%
Test 2=36%	**Test 7**=82%
Test 3=41%	**Test 8**=95%
Test 4=18%	**Test 9**=86%
Test 5=36%	**Test 10**=86%

Q. How well do German Shepherds do?

A. The average score is 5.9 with a standard deviation of 2.1.

Q. How smart is your dog in comparison to other German Shepherds?

A. If your dog obtained a total score of

0–1	Your dog is a very dumb German Shepherd Dog
2–3	Your dog is a dumb German Shepherd Dog
4–8	Your dog is an average German Shepherd Dog
9–10	Your dog is a brilliant German Shepherd Dog

Q. How do the sexes stack up?

A. There are no differences between German Shepherd males and females.

Q. Are city German Shepherds smarter than rural Shepherds?

A. No. There are no differences between city Shepherds and rural Shepherds.

Q. Are registered German Shepherds smarter than non-registered German Shepherds?

A. No. There are no differences in performance.

Q. Do the number of dogs in the dwelling relate to how well German Shepherds do on the Dog Intelligence Test?

A. No. There is no relationship between the number of dogs in the dwelling and how well German Shepherds do on the test.

Q. Do German Shepherds who live in the house do better than those who live outside?

A. No. There are no differences in performance.

Q. Do show German Shepherds do better than others?

A. No. There are no differences in performance.

Q. Do non-kennel German Shepherds do better than kennel Shepherds?

A. No. There are no differences in performance.

Q. Do related dogs (i.e., dogs of the same bloodline) do better than non-related dogs?

A. Yes. Some related dogs' performances were significantly more consistent than non-related dogs' performances and the performances of other groups of related dogs.

Q. Do adult German Shepherds do better than puppies?

A. No. There are no differences in performance.

GREAT DANE

Q. How hard is each test for Great Danes?

A. The best way to answer this is to show the percentage of Great Danes passing each test.

Percentage of Tests Passed

Test 1=90%	**Test 6**= 70%
Test 2=60%	**Test 7**= 80%
Test 3=50%	**Test 8**= 90%
Test 4=50%	**Test 9**= 80%
Test 5=50%	**Test 10**=100%

Q. How well do Great Danes do?

A. The average score is 7.2 with a standard deviation of 2.5.

Q. How smart is your dog in comparison to other Great Danes?

A. If your dog obtained a total score of

0–2	Your dog is a very dumb Great Dane
3–4	Your dog is a dumb Great Dane
5–9	Your dog is an average Great Dane
10	Your dog is a brilliant Great Dane

Q. How do the sexes stack up?

A. There are no differences between Great Dane males and females.

Q. Are city Great Danes smarter than rural Great Danes?

A. There are no differences between city Great Danes and rural Great Danes.

Q. Are registered Great Danes smarter than non-registered Great Danes?

A. No. There are no differences in performance.

Q. Do the number of dogs in the dwelling relate to how well Great Danes do on the Dog Intelligence Test?

A. No. There is no relationship between the number of dogs in the dwelling and how well Great Danes do on the test.

Q. Do Great Danes who live in the house do better than those who live outside?

A. No. There are no differences in performance.

Q. Do show Great Danes do better than others?

A. No. There are no differences in performance.

Q. Do related dogs (i.e., dogs of the same bloodline) do better or worse than non-related dogs?

A. No. There are no differences in performance.

Q. Do altered Great Danes do differently?

A. No. There are no differences in performance.

ST. BERNARD

Q. How hard is each test for St. Bernards?

A. The best way to answer this is to show the percentage of Saint Bernards passing each test.

Percentage of Tests Passed

Test 1=50%	**Test 6**=80%
Test 2=40%	**Test 7**=80%
Test 3=25%	**Test 8**=90%
Test 4=35%	**Test 9**=50%
Test 5=50%	**Test 10**=80%

Q. How well do St. Bernards do?

A. The average score is 5.7 with a standard deviation of 1.5.

Q. How smart is your dog in comparison to other St. Bernards?

A. If your dog obtained a total score of

0–2	Your dog is a very dumb St. Bernard
3–4	Your dog is a dumb St. Bernard
5–7	Your dog is an average St. Bernard
8–9	Your dog is a smart St. Bernard
10	Your dog is a brilliant St. Bernard

Q. How do the sexes stack up?

A. There are no differences between St. Bernard males and females.

SHETLAND SHEEPDOG

G. How hard is each test for Shetland Sheepdogs?

A. The best way to answer this is to show the percentage of Shetland Sheepdogs passing each test.

Percentage of Tests Passed

Test 1=57%	**Test 6**=43%
Test 2=57%	**Test 7**=43%
Test 3=57%	**Test 8**=57%
Test 4=29%	**Test 9**=86%
Test 5=29%	**Test 10**=14%

Q. How well do Shetland Sheepdogs do?

A. The average score is 4.9 with a standard deviation of 1.6.

Q. How smart is your dog in comparison to other Shetland Sheepdogs?

A. If your dog obtained a total score of

0–1   Your dog is a very dumb Shetland Sheepdog
2–3   Your dog is a dumb Shetland Sheepdog
4–7   Your dog is an average Shetland Sheepdog
8   Your dog is a smart Shetland Sheepdog
9–10   Your dog is a brilliant Shetland Sheepdog

Q. How do the sexes stack up?

A. There are no differences between Shetland Sheepdog males and females.

Q. Are registered Shetland Sheepdogs smarter than non-registered Shetland Sheepdogs?

A. No. There are no differences in performance.

Q. Do the number of dogs in the dwelling relate to how well Shetland Sheepdogs do on the Dog Intelligence Test?

A. No. There is no relationship between the number of dogs in the dwelling and how well Shetland Sheepdogs do on the test.

SIBERIAN HUSKY

Q. How hard is each test for Siberians?

A. The best way to answer this is to show the percentage of Siberians passing each test.

Percentage of Tests Passed

Test 1=20%	**Test 6**=30%
Test 2=20%	**Test 7**=50%
Test 3=15%	**Test 8**=60%
Test 4=15%	**Test 9**=45%
Test 5=25%	**Test 10**=50%

Q. How well do Siberians do?

A. The average score is 3.2 with a standard deviation of 1.4.

Q. How smart is your dog in comparison to other Siberians?

A. If your dog obtained a total score of

0	Your dog is a very dumb Siberian Husky
1	Your dog is a dumb Siberian Husky
2–5	Your dog is an average Siberian Husky
6	Your dog is a smart Siberian Husky
7	Your dog is a very smart Siberian Husky
8–10	Your dog is a brilliant Siberian Husky

Q. How do the sexes stack up?

A. There are no differences between Siberian Husky males and females.

TERRIERS

AIREDALE TERRIER

Q. How hard is each test for Airedale Terriers?

A. The best way to answer this is to show the percentage of Airedales passing each test.

Percentage of Tests Passed

Test 1=58%	**Test 6**= 33%
Test 2=42%	**Test 7**= 67%
Test 3=25%	**Test 8**= 92%
Test 4=50%	**Test 9**= 75%
Test 5=42%	**Test 10**=100%

Q. How well do Airedale Terriers do?

A. The average score is 5.8 with a standard deviation of 2.0.

Q. How smart is your dog in comparison to other Airedale Terriers?

A. If your dog obtained a total score of

0–1   Your dog is a very dumb Airedale Terrier
2–3   Your dog is a dumb Airedale Terrier
4–8   Your dog is an average Airedale Terrier
9–10   Your dog is a brilliant Airedale Terrier

Q. How do the sexes stack up?

A. There are no differences between Airedale males and females.

Q. Do the number of dogs in the dwelling relate to how well Airedales do on the Dog Intelligence Test?

A. No. There is no relationship between the number of dogs in the dwelling and how well Airedale Terriers do on the Dog Intelligence Test.

Q. Do Airedale Terriers who live in the house do better than those who live outside?

A. No. There are no differences in performance.

Q. Do housebroken Airedales do better than those who are not housebroken?

A. No. There are no differences in performance.

Q. Do show Airedales do better than others?

A. No. There are no differences in performance.

Q. Do non-kennel Airedale Terriers do better than kennel Airedales?

A. Yes. Non-kennel Airedales do significantly better in performance on the Dog Intelligence Test than kennel Airedales.

Q. Do related dogs (i.e., dogs of the same bloodline) do better than non-related dogs?

A. No. There are no differences in performance.

SCHNAUZER, MINIATURE

Q. How hard is each test for Miniature Schnauzers?

A. The best way to answer this is to show the percentage of Miniature Schnauzers passing each test.

Percentage of Tests Passed

Test 1=60%	**Test 6**=35%
Test 2=35%	**Test 7**=80%
Test 3=40%	**Test 8**=85%
Test 4=35%	**Test 9**=65%
Test 5=40%	**Test 10**=75%

Q. How well do Miniature Schnauzers do?

A. The average score is 5.6 with a standard deviation of 1.3.

Q. How smart is your dog in comparison with other Miniature Schnauzers?

A. If your dog obtained a total score of

0–2	Your dog is a very dumb Miniature Schnauzer
3–4	Your dog is a dumb Miniature Schnauzer
5–7	Your dog is an average Miniature Schnauzer
8	Your dog is a smart Miniature Schnauzer
9–10	Your dog is a brilliant Miniature Schnauzer

Q. How do the sexes stack up?

A. There are no differences between Miniature Schnauzer males and females.

WEST HIGHLAND WHITE TERRIER

Q. How hard is each test for West Highland White Terriers?

A. The best way to answer this is to show the percentage of Westies passing each test.

Percentage of Tests Passed

Test 1=40%	**Test 6**=40%
Test 2=20%	**Test 7**=40%
Test 3=40%	**Test 8**=60%
Test 4=20%	**Test 9**=40%
Test 5=20%	**Test 10**=60%

Q. How well do West Highland White Terriers do?

A. The average score is 4.0 with a standard deviation of .63.

Q. How smart is your dog in comparison to other West Highland White Terriers?

A. If your dog obtained a total score of

0–2   Your dog is a very dumb West Highland White Terrier

3   Your dog is a dumb West Highland White Terrier

4–5   Your dog is an average West Highland White Terrier

6   Your dog is a very smart West Highland White Terrier

7–10   Your dog is a brilliant West Highland White Terrier

Q. How do the sexes stack up?

A. There are no differences between West Highland White Terrier males and females.

Q. Do the number of dogs in the dwelling relate to how well Westies do on the Dog Intelligence Test?

A. No. There is no relationship between the number of dogs in the dwelling and how well West Highland White Terriers do on the test.

TOYS

CHIHUAHUA (SMOOTH-COATED)

Q. How hard is each test for Chihuahuas?

A. The best way to answer this is to show the percentage of Chihuahuas passing each test.

Percentage of Tests Passed

Test 1 = 30%	**Test 6** = 10%
Test 2 = 40%	**Test 7** = 15%
Test 3 = 35%	**Test 8** = 20%
Test 4 = 30%	**Test 9** = 5%
Test 5 = 30%	**Test 10** = 5%

Q. How well do Chihuahuas do?

A. The average score is 2.2 with a standard deviation of .7.

Q. How smart is your dog in comparison to other Chihuahuas?

A. If your dog obtained a total score of

0	Your dog is a very dumb Chihuahua
1	Your dog is a dumb Chihuahua
2–3	Your dog is an average Chihuahua
4	Your dog is a smart Chihuahua
5–10	Your dog is a brilliant Chihuahua

Q. How do the sexes stack up?

A. There are no differences between Chihuahua males and females.

PEKINGESE

Q. How hard is each test for Pekingese?

A. The best way to answer this is to show the percentage of Pekingese passing each test.

Percentage of Tests Passed

Test 1=40%	**Test 6**=35%
Test 2=65%	**Test 7**=30%
Test 3=55%	**Test 8**=60%
Test 4=40%	**Test 9**=65%
Test 5=60%	**Test 10**=65%

Q. How well do Pekingese do?

A. The average score is 5.3 with a standard deviation of 1.4.

Q. How smart is your dog in comparison to other Pekingese?

A. If your dog obtained a total score of

0–2	Your dog is a very dumb Pekingese
3	Your dog is a dumb Pekingese
4–7	Your dog is an average Pekingese
8	Your dog is a smart Pekingese
9–10	Your dog is a brilliant Pekingese

Q. How do the sexes stack up?

A. There are no differences between Pekingese males and females.

POMERANIAN

Q. How hard is each test for Pomeranians?

A. The best way to answer this is to show the percentage of Pomeranians passing each test.

Percentage of Tests Passed

Test 1=20%	**Test 6**=15%
Test 2=25%	**Test 7**=20%
Test 3=20%	**Test 8**=40%
Test 4=30%	**Test 9**=30%
Test 5=15%	**Test 10**=60%

Q. How well do Pomeranians do?

A. The average score is 2.8 with a standard deviation of 1.1.

Q. How smart is your dog in comparison to other Pomeranians?

A. If your dog obtained a total score of

0	Your dog is a very dumb Pomeranian
1	Your dog is a dumb Pomeranian
2–4	Your dog is an average Pomeranian
5	Your dog is a smart Pomeranian
6	Your dog is a very smart Pomeranian
7–10	Your dog is a brilliant Pomeranian

Q. How do the sexes stack up?

A. There are no differences between Pomeranian males and females.

TOY POODLE

Q. How hard is each test for Toy Poodles?

A. The best way to answer this is to show the percentage of Toy Poodles passing each test.

Percentage of Tests Passed

Test 1=50%	**Test 6**=60%
Test 2=40%	**Test 7**=65%
Test 3=45%	**Test 8**=90%
Test 4=45%	**Test 9**=50%
Test 5=50%	**Test 10**=80%

Q. How well do Toy Poodles do?

A. The average score is 5.8 with a standard deviation of 1.0.

Q. How smart is your dog in comparison to other Toy Poodles?

A. If your dog obtained a total score of

0–3	Your dog is a very dumb Toy Poodle
4	Your dog is a dumb Toy Poodle
5–7	Your dog is an average Toy Poodle
8	Your dog is a smart Toy Poodle
9	Your dog is a very smart Toy Poodle
10	Your dog is a brilliant Toy Poodle

Q. How do the sexes stack up?

A. There are no differences between Toy Poodle males and females.

PUG

Q. How hard is each test for Pugs?

A. The best way to answer this is to show the percentage of Pugs passing each test.

Percentage of Tests Passed

Test 1=40%	**Test 6**=30%
Test 2=50%	**Test 7**=35%
Test 3=55%	**Test 8**=60%
Test 4=40%	**Test 9**=35%
Test 5=50%	**Test 10**=20%

Q. How well do Pugs do?

A. The average score is 4.2 with a standard deviation of .8.

Q. How smart is your dog in comparison to other Pugs?

A. If your dog obtained a total score of

0–2	Your dog is a very dumb Pug
3	Your dog is a dumb Pug
4–5	Your dog is an average Pug
6	Your dog is a smart Pug
7	Your dog is a very smart Pug
8–10	Your dog is a brilliant Pug

Q. How do the sexes stack up?

A. There are no differences between Pug males and females.

SILKY TERRIER

Q. How hard is each test for Silky Terriers?

A. The best way to answer this is to show the percentage of Silky Terriers passing each test.

Percentage of Tests Passed

Test 1=50%	**Test 6**=60%
Test 2=60%	**Test 7**=45%
Test 3=40%	**Test 8**=95%
Test 4=45%	**Test 9**=55%
Test 5=40%	**Test 10**=80%

Q. How well do Silky Terriers do?

A. The average score is 5.8 with a standard deviation .of 1.3.

Q. How smart is your dog in comparison to other Silky Terriers?

A. If your dog obtained a total score of

0–3	Your dog is a very dumb Silky Terrier
4	Your dog is a dumb Silky Terrier
5–7	Your dog is an average Silky Terrier
8	Your dog is a smart Silky Terrier
9–10	Your dog is a brilliant Silky Terrier

Q. How do the sexes stack up?

A. There are no differences between Silky Terrier males and females.

NON-SPORTING DOGS

BULLDOG

W. How hard is each test for Bulldogs?

A. The best way to answer this is to show the percentage of Bulldogs passing each test.

Percentage of Tests Passed

Test 1=85%	**Test 6**= 90%
Test 2=80%	**Test 7**= 95%
Test 3=70%	**Test 8**= 95%
Test 4=80%	**Test 9**= 45%
Test 5=90%	**Test 10**=100%

Q. How well do Bulldogs do?

A. The average score is 8.4 with a standard deviation of 1.3.

Q. How smart is your dog in comparison to other Bulldogs?

A. If your dog obtained a total score of

0–5	Your dog is a very dumb Bulldog
6–7	Your dog is a dumb Bulldog
8–9	Your dog is an average Bulldog
10	Your dog is a brilliant Bulldog

Q. How do the sexes stack up?

A. There are no differences between Bulldog males and females.

LHASA APSO

Q. How hard is each test for Lhasa Apsos?

A. The best way to answer this is to show the percentage of Lhasa Apsos passing each test.

Percentage of Tests Passed

Test 1=40%	**Test 6**=40%
Test 2=35%	**Test 7**=80%
Test 3=30%	**Test 8**=95%
Test 4=25%	**Test 9**=75%
Test 5=25%	**Test 10**=45%

Q. How well do Lhasa Apsos do?

A. The average score is 4.7 with a standard deviation of 2.2.

Q. How smart is your dog in comparison to other Lhasa Apsos?

A. If your dog obtained a total score of

0	Your dog is a very dumb Lhasa Apso
1–2	Your dog is a dumb Lhasa Apso
3–7	Your dog is an average Lhasa Apso
8–9	Your dog is a smart Lhasa Apso
10	Your dog is a brilliant Lhasa Apso

Q. How do the sexes stack up?

A. There are no differences between Lhasa Apso males and females.

MINIATURE POODLE

Q. How hard is each test for Miniature Poodles?

A. The best way to answer this is to show the percentage of Miniature Poodles passing each test.

Percentage of Tests Passed

Test 1=63%	**Test 6**=38%
Test 2=50%	**Test 7**=75%
Test 3=63%	**Test 8**=75%
Test 4=75%	**Test 9**=75%
Test 5=63%	**Test 10**=50%

Q. How well do Miniature Poodles do?

A. The average score is 6.1 with a standard deviation of 2.5.

Q. How smart is your dog in comparison to other Miniature Poodles?

A. If your dog obtained a total score of

0–1	Your dog is a very dumb Miniature Poodle
2–3	Your dog is a dumb Miniature Poodle
4–9	Your dog is an average Miniature Poodle
10	Your dog is a brilliant Miniature Poodle

Q. How do the sexes stack up?

A. There are no differences between Miniature Poodle males and females.

Q. Are registered Miniature Poodles smarter than non-registered Miniature Poodles?

A. No. There are no differences in performance.

Q. Do the number of dogs in the dwelling relate to how well Miniature Poodles do on the Dog Intelligence Test?

A. Yes. Miniature Poodles do significantly better on the Dog Intelligence Test when three or more dogs are in the dwelling. Performances for one or two dogs in the dwelling are no different.

Q. Do altered Miniature Poodles do differently?

A. No. There are no differences in performance.

STANDARD POODLE

Q. How hard is each test for Standard Poodles?

A. The best way to answer this is to show the percentage of Standard Poodles passing each test.

Percentage of Tests Passed

Test 1=80%	**Test 6**= 80%
Test 2=85%	**Test 7**= 95%
Test 3=90%	**Test 8**= 95%
Test 4=95%	**Test 9**= 90%
Test 5=95%	**Test 10**=100%

Q. How well do Standard Poodles do?

A. The average score is 8.8 with a standard deviation of .6 .

Q. How smart is your dog in comparison to other Standard Poodles?

A. If your dog obtained a total score of

0–8	Your dog is a dumb Standard Poodle
9	Your dog is an average Standard Poodle
10	Your dog is a brilliant Standard Poodle

Q. How do the sexes stack up?

A. There are no differences between Standard Poodle males and females.

SCHIPPERKE

Q. How hard is each test for Schipperkes?

A. The best way to answer this is to show the percentage of Schipperkes passing each test.

Percentage of Tests Passed

Test 1=50%	**Test 6**=50%
Test 2=60%	**Test 7**=60%
Test 3=65%	**Test 8**=90%
Test 4=45%	**Test 9**=70%
Test 5=55%	**Test 10**=50%

Q. How well do Schipperkes do?

A. The average score is 5.7 with a standard deviation of 1.5.

Q. How smart is your dog in comparison to other Schipperkes?

A. If your dog obtained a total score of

0–2	Your dog is a very dumb Schipperke
3–4	Your dog is a dumb Schipperke
5–7	Your dog is an average Schipperke
8–9	Your dog is a smart Schipperke
10	Your dog is a brilliant Schipperke

Q. How do the sexes stack up?

A. There are no differences between Schipperke males and females.

·MISCELLANEOUS

AUSTRALIAN SHEPHERD

Q. How hard is each test for Australian Shepherds?

A. The best way to answer this is to show the percentage of Australian Shepherds passing each test.

Percentage of Tests Passed

Test 1=50%	**Test 6**=80%
Test 2=40%	**Test 7**=85%
Test 3=45%	**Test 8**=90%
Test 4=80%	**Test 9**=75%
Test 5=70%	**Test 10**=80%

Q. How well do Australian Shepherds do?

A. The average score is 6.8 with a standard deviation of 1.5.

Q. How smart is your dog in comparison to other Australian Shepherds?

A. If your dog obtained a total score of

0–3	Your dog is a very dumb Australian Shepherd
4–5	Your dog is a dumb Australian Shepherd
6–8	Your dog is an average Australian Shepherd
9–10	Your dog is a brilliant Australian Shepherd

Q. How do the sexes stack up?

A. There are no differences between Australian Shepherd males and females.